RUSSIAN SOUVENIR

L. N. Soloviova

MATRYOSHKA

INTERBOOK BUSINESS

Moscow, 1997

Photography by
Eugeny Gavrilov

Design by
Ludmila Pertseva

Cover design by
Yuri Leonov

Printed in Slovenia by Gorenjski Tisk, Kranj

ISBN 5-89164-016-3

MATRYOSHKA

*T*he matryoshka is the most famous Russian souvenir which is popular with everyone, it is considered to be a phenomenon in the world culture. This idea is recognised not only by connoisseurs of the language, history and culture of this country but also by those who just begin their acquaintance with Russia.

Matryoshka has become sort of a formula of a cultural phenomenon which is unique and has a meaning of its own.

It is hard to imagine now that only about one hundred years ago matryoshka has not existed at all. The first Russian matryoshka appeared only at the end of the 19th century. It was greatly acclaimed as one of the all-embracing image of Russia, symbol of Russian folk art.

The end of the 19th century in Russia was a period of great economic and cultural development, a period of rising national identity. It was the time of great interest in Russian culture generally and particularly in Russian art. A new artistic trend known as 'Russian style' appeared. Such artists as V. M. Vasnetsov, K. A. Somov, M. A. Vrubel, N. K. Rerih, V. A. Serov, F. A. Maliavin, K. A. Korovin, S. V. Maliutin were possessed by the idea of creation of a new style where Russian national traditions would revive. They understood that it was necessary to find unity and harmony of the past and present in art and life. Due to their efforts at the end of the 19th century and at the beginning of the 20th century artistic creative units started to spring up. They can be called spiritual and cultural centres of Russia.

Abramtsevo artistic unit of S. I. Mamontov was part of this cultural trend of the development and revival of Russian traditional national art. S. I. Mamontov (1841-1918) belonged to the famous merchant family, he was an industrialist and a patron of the arts. Mamontov was one of the first men who patronised artists who were possessed by the idea of the creation of a new Russian style. Art studios were established in his Abramtsevo estate near Moscow.

Professional artists worked along with folk craftsmen who preserved aesthetic and age-long skills of folk art. The Mamontovs dealt with enlightenment

and art collecting. Peasant toys were in their collection of folk art. Special attention was paid to the revival and development of folk peasant toys.

That was a great merit of the family of Anatoly Ivanovich Mamontov (1839-1905), the brother of S. I. Mamontov. This family owned workshop 'Children's Education' where various toys for children were made and sold. So-called ethnographic dolls dressed in folk festive costumes of inhabitants of various Russian regions (*gubernias* and *uezds*)

S. Maliutin (painting), V. Zviozdochkin (fashioning)
8-piece matryoshka
Moscow, workshop 'Children's Education'
Late 1890s
APMT

were especially distinguished. A. I. Mamontov, a publisher, translator and owner of a printing-house, collector of Russian paintings as well as his brother S. I. Mamontov, was a remarkable and active person, who was always surrounded by professional artists, artisans and folk craftsmen.

A. I. Mamontov offered jobs in his studio to highly qualified creative toy makers who had initiative and fantasy. There were various samples of toys from different countries in the workshop to broaden toy makers outlook and to develop their creative fantasy. Oriental art and Japanese fine and applied art in particular was very fashionable at that time.*

Thus, a famous predecessor and prototype of Russian matryoshka was brought to Russia from the Island of Honshu. It was a figurine of a good-natured bold headed old man, Buddhist sage by the name of Fukuruma. The doll contained some other figurines nestled inside one another. There was a stamp on the figurine's butt-end: made in Japan. By the way the Japanese claimed that the first doll of such a type on the Island of Honshu was made by unknown Russian monk. Now the Fukuruma figurine is kept in the Artistic Pedagogical Museum of Toys (APMT) in Sergiev Posad.

---

* The exhibition of Japanese Art, opened in December 1896, in St. Petersburg, contributed to this a lot. A. P. Ostroumova-Lebedeva recalled afterwards that she was greatly impressed by '...sharp realism along with the mysticism, definite style and simplification'.

8

The first Russian matryoshka also has a stamp: 'Children's Education' workshop.

The legendary matryoshka was made in the workshop of A. I. Mamontov. The hereditary toy maker, Vassiliy Petrovich Zviozdochkin was entrusted to turn this toy. The first samples of matryoshkas were painted by S. V. Maliutin. At that time he also illustrated books for children.

D. Pichugin
12-piece matryoshka
'Boyarin'
Sergiev Posad. 1903-1910
APMT

That's why illustrations and the first samples of matryoshkas have a lot in common.

Perhaps, S. V. Maliutin and V. P. Zviozdochkin didn't think that the first Russian wooden doll within smaller dolls made by them would be very popular all over the world. They didn't think that their matryoshka would be a symbol of some magic secret and mysterious Russian soul.

The makers of the first Russian matryoshka were really talented and unique people. When great Rilke visited Russia at the turn of the 19th-20th centuries, he noted that ancient crafts still existed in Russia: artistic embroidery on towels and clothes or carved wooden items. S. V. Maliutin was the best connoisseur of Russian folk art. Being an artist he used the colours and the style of ancient Russian folk art in his own work. S. V. Maliutin belonged to the

A. Shishkin
Matryoshka **'A Boyar Maid'**
Matryoshka **'A Boyar Man'**
Sergiev Posad. 1920s
APMT

old Russian merchants family, his experience and knowledge of Russian ancient and folk art came not only from archaeological and ethnographic sources. Due to his talent and intuition he was the first of the artists who united folk and professional art. His matryoshka was a light, elegant, spontaneous figurine of a round faced peasant young girl dressed in colourful scarf, an embroidered shirt , sarafan (Russian national costume) and apron. She was holding a black rooster in her hands.

Russian wooden dolls within smaller dolls were called matryoshka. In provincial Russia before the revolution the name Matryona or

V. Ivanov
8-piece matryoshka
'Grandfather Turnip'
Sergiev Posad. 1903-1904
AMPT

Egg-shaped matryoshka
'A Peasant Woman'
Sergiev Posad. 1900-1914
APTM

Matriyosha was a very popular female name. It was derived from the Latin root 'mater' which means 'mother'. This name was associated with the image of a mother of a big family who was very healthy and had a portly figure. Subsequently, it became a symbolic name and was used specially to describe brightly painted wooden dolls made in such a way that they could be taken apart to reveal smaller dolls fitting inside one another.

Even now matryoshka is considered to be a symbol of motherhood and fertility. A mother doll with numerous dolls- children perfectly expresses the oldest symbol of human culture.

The first Russian matryoshka turned by

Craftsman Sharpanov
8-piece matryoshka
'An Old Man'
Sergiev Posad.
Early 20th century
AMPT

12

Vassily Zviozdochkin and painted by Sergey Maliutin contained 8 pieces: a girl with a black rooster was followed by a boy and then by a girl again and so on. All figurines were different from each other, the last one was a figurine of a baby wrapped in diaper.

It was quite easy for Russian craftsmen who had had a considerable experience in turning wooden objects which fitted inside each other (for example, Easter eggs) to work out the matryoshka making technology.

Craftsman Baranov
8-piece matryoshka
Sergiev Posad. 1900-1914
APMT

The basic technique of matryoshka making remains unchanged. As a rule matryoshkas are made from lime, birch, alder and aspen. Lime is the most abundant material. The trees chosen to manufacture matryoshkas are cut down at the beginning of Spring, usually in April when the trees are full of sap. The felled trees are stripped of their bark leaving a few rings to prevent the wood from cracking . The logs prepared in this way with their butt-ends smeared over are arranged in piles with a clearance between them to allow aeration.

The logs are kept in the open air for two years. Only an experience master can tell when the material is ready. Then the logs are cut into workpieces for matryoshkas. Every workpiece can be turned as many as 15 times before the matryoshka will be ready. Making a doll on a turning lathe requires high skills , an ability to work with a beguilingly small set of tools—a knife and chisels of various length and shape. The smallest figurine which cannot be taken apart usually is made first. The bottom part of the next figurine which can be taken apart is turned first. Then a workpiece is turned to reach the necessary size and the top end is removed. Then the ring is made to fit on it the upper part of the matryoshka and then its lower part can be made. Then the matryoshka's head is turned and the necessary amount of wood is removed from within the matryoshka's head to slip on the upper ring. All these operations do not involve any

7-piece matryoshka
'Gipsy Woman'
Sergiev Posad. 1900-1914
APMT

The upper part of the matryoshka is stuck on to its lower part, dries and tightens the ring so it sits securely in place. When the turning work is over, a snow white doll is thoroughly cleaned, primed with starchy glue to make the surface ideally smooth and to prevent the paint making smudges and then dried. Now it is ready to be painted. The first Russian matryoshka was poked and painted with gouache and covered with varnish by S. V. Maliutin.

Until late 1890s matryoshkas were manufactured in 'Children's Education' workshop in Moscow. When it was closed the tradition of matryoshka making was maintained in the training workshop in Sergiev Posad, Russian toy-making centre. Soon large-scale production of matryoshkas was launched there. The work-shops developed the type of matryoshka which is

known as Sergiev Posad or Zagorsk matryoshka. (In 1930 the city was renamed Zagorsk. Now it has its historical name back).

Sergiev Posad is situated 73km (45.5 miles) from Moscow. It has grown up around famous Trinity-St. Sergius Monastery. In 1340 the monk St. Sergius Radonezhsky founded a small temple

lost in the midst of the wild forests. In time it was developed into the biggest monastery of Russia.

Arts and crafts were flourished in the towns and villages which surrounded the monastery. Wooden toys which were known as 'Trinity' toys became particular popular. According to the legend the first 'Trinity' wooden toy was made by the Prior of the Monastery, Sergius Radonezhsky.

V. Ivanov
12-piece matryoshka
Sergiev Posad. 1903-1904
APTM

He personally gave the toys to the children.

The pilgrims who came to the Monastery from all over the country were quite happy to buy toys for their children. Even the Tsar's children played with wooden 'Trinity' toys—wooden harnesses, small bowls and spoons. They were purchased in Sergiev Posad where Russian tsars went to pray with their families.

7-piece matryoshka
Sergiev Posad. 1920s
APMT

Wooden toys, a peasant girl in *kokoshnik* (peasant head-dress), a dancing *muzhik* (peasant man) and well-dressed ladies and hussars came down to us from the end of the 18th century beginning of the 19th century. These toys were real wooden painted figurines. Wooden painted carved ladies and hussars had individuality and looked like real characters.

The new wooden toy, matryoshka, painted by professianoal artists in Moscow workshop had a secound birth in this old toy-making center with numerous workshops where skilful hereditary masters worked. In 1900 Russian matryoshka took part in World Exhibition in Paris where it got a medal and became internationally known. The first foreign orders for wooden dolls were made at that time.

It could be fulfilled only by skilled craftsmen of Sergiev Posad. In 1904 A. I. Mamontov sold his shop to S. T. Morozov. Then S. T. Morosov opened a branch of Crafts Museum and a workshop in Sergiev Posad. Vasiliy Zviozdochkin, the turner, who made the first Russian matryoshka came from Moscow to work in this workshop. On A. I. Mamontov's orders many matryoshka samples were made in the workshop.

The art of making and painting matryoshkas in Sergiev Posad in the early decades of the 20th century was so original that it set a trend of matryoshka painting in Russia for many years ahead. At that time the main technique of matryoshka painting was set in Sergiev Posad. The distinctive feature of this technique was the real style of painting.

Sergiev Posad was a colourful, truly Russian town. The Monastery lent a unique peculiarity to it. The huge market place in front of the Monastery was almost always full of different people: merchants, monks, pilgrims and craftsmen were milling around.

The first matryoshkas of Sergiev Posad portrayed this colourful life: young girls dressed in Russian sarafans carrying baskets, scythes,

V. Ivanov
Matryoshka **'A Peasant woman'**
Sergiev Posad. 1903-1904
APTM

bunches of flowers or dressed in winter short fur coats and scarves; old believer women in their sectarian clothes; a bride and a bridegroom holding candles in their hands; a shepherd with a pipe; an old man with a lush beard. At the early period of Sergiev Posad technique development along with female images male images were made as well.

Sometimes matryoshka represented the whole family with numerous children and members of household. Some matryoshkas were devoted to historical themes. They portrayed boyars and their wives, Russian nobility of the 17th century and legendary Russian *bogatyrs* (warriors). Some matryoshkas were devoted to the book characters. For instance, in 1909 to celebrate the centenary of Gogol's birth, a series of matryoshkas portrayed the characters of his books: Taras Bulba, Plyushkin, Governor. In 1912, to celebrate the centenary of the Patriotic War against Napoleon matryoshkas portrayed Kutuzov and Napoleon whose figurines contained smaller figurines of their field commanders. Some matryoshkas borrowed their subjects from folk tales and folk heroic sagas: Tsar Dadon and Princess Swan from Pushkin's tales, 'The Little Humpback Horse' from Yershov's tale, some characters from Krilov's fable 'The Quartet'.

Along with painted decorations, some matryoshkas featured poker work. Usually poker work was applied to outline the ornament of the whole doll, its clothes, face, hands, scarf and hair.

Matryoshka-shaped case
'A Calf in the Chamberlain's Costume'
Sergiev Posad. 1900-1914
APTM

I. Prokhorov
8-piece matryoshka
'Napoleon's Headquarters'
Sergiev Posad. 1912
APMT

Sometimes the poker pattern was supplemented with a slight tinging of minor decorative details, for instance, a bunch of flowers in the matryoshka's hands or the floral design on the scarf. The traditional matryoshka was also a subject of some experiment. Some figurines were given a shape of an old Russian helmet or a cone. But these 'innovations' were not that

I. Prokhorov
8-piece matryoshka
'Kutuzov's Headquarters'
Sergiev Posad. 1912
APMT

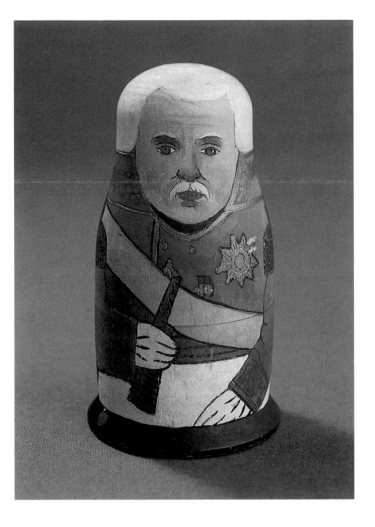

8-piece matryoshka
'Hetman'
Sergiev Posad
Early 20th century
APMT

4-piece matryoshka (Vrubel matryoshka)
Sergiev Posad. 1903-1910
APTM

E. Novshchentseva
5-piece matryoshka **'Bread and Salt'**
Sergiev Posad, 'Souvenir' factory
1996

18-piece matryoshka
Zagorsk. 'The Workers' and Peasants'
Red Army Artel'
1920-1930
APTM

popular with customers who preferred the traditional matryoshka.

Though the first painted matryoshkas of Sergiev Posad were quite expensive, they quickly won admiration of adults and children. Four years after the successful presentation of Russian painted matryoshka at the World Exhibition in Paris in 1900, 'The Russian Craftsmen' partnership opened a permanent shop in Paris where orders came to make matryoshkas. In 1911 such orders for matryoshkas came from 14 countries. The Russian matryoshka was so popular that foreign businessmen started to manufacture *a la Russe* dolls.

Such dolls were on sale in Germany, France and other countries but the trend petered out because it did not have national soil. On the contrary, the art of the Russian matryoshka of Sergiev Posad was developed further. In 1911 the list of the products of Sergiev Zemstvo training workshop included 21 types of matryoshkas: they had different sizes, painting and different amount of pieces. The matryoshkas of Sergiev Posad consisted of 2 to 24 pieces. The most

E. Shatova
13-piece matryoshka. 1994
13-piece matryoshka. 1989
12-piece matryoshka. 1987
Sergiev Posad, 'Souvenir' facrory

popular matryoshkas consisted of 3, 8 and 12 pieces. In 1913 a 48-piece matryoshka made by N. Bulichev was displayed at the Exhibition of Toys in St. Petersburg.

In the initial period of Russian matryoshka development, a turner played a very important role. Highly skilled masters turned matryoshkas with very thin sides which was considered to be a special art of matryoshka turning. Apparently, painting was secondary. Professional artists who painted the first turned matryoshkas didn't treat it seriously enough. It was sort of entertainment. There are some matryoshkas—caricatures in the Museum Estate Polenovo.

During the first two decades matryoshkas

30

N. Ivantsova (painting)
V. Bulashov (fashioning)
25-piece matryoshka
Sergiev Posad
Center of Sergiev Traditional Culture
(CSTC)
1996

'Marya' case inlaid with Vyatka straw
'Souvenir' factory. 1996

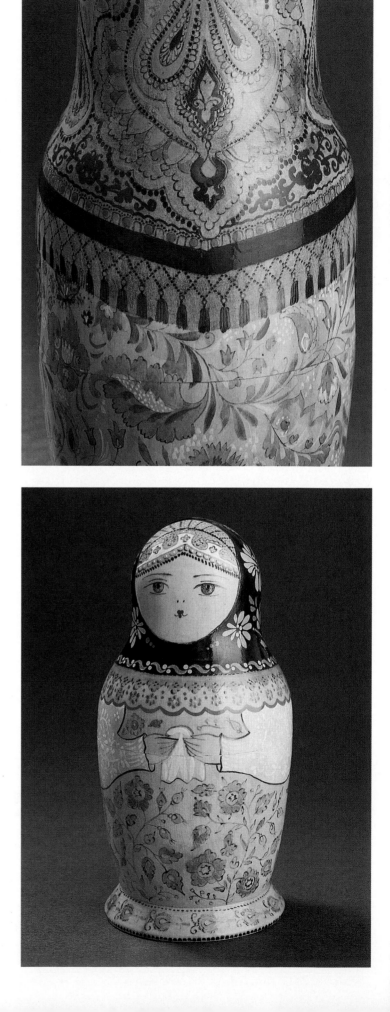

I. Marachiova
14-piece matryoshka (with a fragment)
Zagorsk. 1984
APTM

ON PAGE 33:
I. Marachiova
12-piece matryoshka
Zagorsk. 1985
APTM

were rather diverse. The first group included matryoshkas painted in Russian style or more generally in modern style by professional artists. The first matryoshka painted by S. V. Maliutin represented a figurine of a bull-calf, dressed in the chamberlain costume, decorated by poker work with a characteristic ornament in the modern style.

The second group included matryoshkas made in the independent workshops of Sergiev Posad. They were painted by the artists from the local icon painting school.

In the first decades of the 20th century craftsmen of Sergiev Posad developed their own technique of painting and decoration based on deep national traditions. This sincere, naive, unsubtle art impressed everybody and was understood by all. Due to the fact that this art was based on the national culture, it was full of coarse force and expression and was different from exquisite matryoshkas painted by professional artists. 'An Old Man', 'Matryoshka with a Goose', 'Matryoshka with a Basket' and others belong to this group.

32

O. Provada
8-piece matryoshka
'Motherhood'
Sergiev Posad, 'Souvenir' factory.
1995

Folk art tradition was very important in the development of the Russian matryoshka style. Due to the widest layer of folk culture, matryoshka continued to exist even after Russian style, developed by Russian professional artists was forgotten. Icon painters of Sergiev Posad contributed a lot to matryoshka pictorial style. Anthropomorphism, in other words, resemblance to a human being of the Russian 'take apart' doll turned out to be the continuation of ancient Rus-

sian art tradition. An artist focused mainly on the figure of a person, his or her face.

This tradition of Russian ancient art came from Byzantine Empire which had borrowed it from the artists of antiquity. The great Russian painter, V. A. Favorsky said that ancient Russian painting '...is a direct continuation of great Greek art and at the same time it has deep Russian national roots'. The connection of certain early type of the matryoshkas of Sergiev Posad

O. Provada
7-piece matryoshka
'Spring'
Sergiev Posad, 'Souvenir' factory
1996

S. Nechayev (painting), S. Bilibin (fashioning)
15-piece matryoshka **'Folk Handicrafts'**
Sergiev Posad. 1996

with the traditions of the local icon painting school is confirmed both stylistically and virtually. Along with the icons, matryoshkas were painted as well in the icon painting school of Sergiev Posad.

Such matryoshkas as 'Yermak', 'Stepan Razin' were painted in R. S. Busigin's workshop. Icon painter D. N. Pichugin painted 'Baltic Type' matryoshkas. The sons of a painter A. I. Sorokin of Trinity - St. Sergius Monastery painted matryoshkas as well. The Ivanov brothers who had the most famous matryoshka workshop used to make icon frames. Many hereditary families of toy painters of Sergiev Posad were connected in one way or another with the local icon painting school.

Great Russian thinker of the early 20th century Vassily Vassilievich Rozanov noted: '...folk element is full of seriousness, full of sense. The people have lived through and are still living through the deepest calamities of the soul; they are very observant; they think hard'. All this explains the appearance of a new kind of folk art—painted matryoshka.

Initially matryoshkas were quite diverse: they portrayed not only female characters but also male ones. There were some ethnographic matryoshkas: Samoyed (Eskimo), Gipsy Woman, Armenian Man, Turk, Chinese, Lithuanians, Tartar Family, Ukrainian and so on.

The matryoshkas portraying certain estates and characterising certain types of activities formed a separate group: numerous boyars, scribes, warriors, policemen, tailors, cooks, waiters, soldiers, artists, Persian Shahs. Some matryoshkas portrayed different characters from books especially from the books of Gogol and Pushkin. However, gradually female characters became the main type of matryoshkas. The traditions of making special matryoshka proportions (1:2, i.e. the ratio between a matryoshka's width to its height) were worked out. Initially such proportions were typical for female and male characters.

The first painters of Sergiev Posad who made matryoshkas continued icon painting traditions: they paid their special attention to the

O. Rozhdestvenskaya
8-piece matryoshka **'Holiday'**
Sergiev Posad, 'Souvenir' factory
1996

N. Antonova
3-piece matryoshka **'Surprise'**
Sergiev Posad. 1994
Private collection

37

matryoshka's face. The matryoshka painters were divided into two groups: the painters who paid their special attention to matryoshka's face and the painters who paid their special attention to matryoshka's clothes. Actually it has existed since the time of Russian ancient icon painting traditions. The clothes were painted by women and faces were painted by men at the final stage of the matryoshka decoration. The faces of the early matryoshkas of Sergiev Posad were oval and strict. The heads of many matryoshkas were greatly enlarged that's why the face dominated the body. These matryoshkas look primitive because of this disproportion but at the same time they are very expressive. The manner of painting is bit coarse.

Early painted matryoshkas attract us by sincerity and naivety of perception of the world. They say that the famous film director

S. A. Gerasimov once asked his students what a woman was. Having heard different answers he said: 'A woman is a mother'.

The art of Russian painted matryoshka develops exactly the same idea about female image.

As the time went on female image of the matryoshkas of earlier period transformed from an

individual type to the typical image which was called later the image of Sergiev Posad.

In 1910 'Artisan-Artist' artel was set up in Sergiev Posad. In 1913 training workshops which produced matryoshkas became a part of this artel. In 1920s the matryoshka makers artel was renamed 'The Workers' and Peasants' Red Army Artel'. In 1928 it became toy factory #1 which exists till the present time.

The history of Russian painted matryoshkas

8-piece matryoshka
'A Girl with a Chicken'
Sergiev Posad, 'Sergiev Toy'
factory. 1996

has three periods. The first one starts with the birth of the Russian matryoshka and lasts until the beginning of 1930s. This period may be described as the time of free work of artisans. The second period which started in the mid 1930s and lasted till late 1980s, was marked as the factory manufacture of matryoshkas when the craftsmen worked together at the state enterprises.

Finally, the third period began at the beginning of 1990s when the free market of matryoshka manufacture and sale triumphed. It was the time of so-called author's matryoshka.

The artistic destiny of the first period matryoshka was quite lamentable. As early as on November 15, 1923 in Moscow the Committee of the Arts and Crafts Museum drawn a writing off act of the exhibits which according to the committee members, did not correspond with the high artistic level, they were not ideologically consistent and were not relics of the past. The matryoshkas were the main part of these exhi-

bits: peasant women, tailors, policemen, scribes, beggars, bakers, mermaids, wood goblins, grenadiers, Chinese, Persians, Jews and so on.

Gradually, all this diversity of matryoshkas was reduced to a certain female image. During the Soviet period the matryoshkas of Zagorsk had academic simplicity and ornamental linear stylisation.

During the third period the matryoshkas of Sergiev Posad came back to their roots. They have possibly lost their original graphic refinement, a characteristic of the works of Chief Artist of Zagorsk factory #1 S. L. Nechaev, but they have gained special graphic ingenuousness which can be found in the works of E. Latisheva and L. Ovchinnikova, masters of the Traditional Culture Centre of Sergiev Posad. The Centre, set up in 1990, was given a task to come back to the roots of artistic handicrafts industry of Sergiev Posad, its artistic and technological traditions and organisational principles.

Sergievskaya Igrushka ('Sergiev Toy') factory, set up in 1995, which works according to the principle of handicraft artels of 1900-1930s became the production base of the Centre. 'Sergievskaya Igrushka' revives the main kinds of the old handicraft toys of Sergiev Posad: papier-mache toys, traditional splinter toys, turning and joiner's wares, made by painting over poker work, and of course, painted matryoshkas.

Along with traditional types of matryoshkas, special attention is paid to author's matryoshkas. The works of E. Latisheva and L. Ovchinniko-

ON PAGE 43:
O. Kiseliova
10-piece matryoshka
'Abramtsevo Nights'
Khotkovo. 1996

ON PAGE 45:
O. Kiseliova
10-piece matryoshka
'Abramtsevo Nights'
View from behind

42

...va are the most interesting. The main subject for these painters is the image of Russian woman-mother. Their female images are extremely strong and expressive. These matryoshkas have something in common with the spontaneity and primitiveness of natural origins.

'Souvenir' was set up on the basis of artistic industrial workshops. Since 1940s the painters and craftsmen of these workshops have developed samples for factory production of matryoshkas. Now the painters of 'Souvenir' continue the best traditions of making the matryoshkas of Sergiev Posad and develop the new themes and methods of matryoshka painting. One of the strongest points of 'Souvenir' matryoshka is its refined graphic elaboration.

In 1918 the Museum of Russian and Foreign Toys was opened in Sergiev Posad. The first Russian matryoshka made by S. V. Maliutin is a part of the Museum's collection. Soon afterwards the Toys Research Institute was organised there as well. The remarkable samples of toys were created in this institute including a 42-piece matryoshka. A 60-piece matryoshka is considered to be the biggest one among the matryoshkas of Sergiev Posad. It was turned by Mokeev in 1967. The matryoshka of Sergiev Posad has its own peculiarities: its top part flows smoothly into the thicker lower part; it is painted with gouache and has a varnish surface. In spite of, or perhaps because of the popularity of the matryoshkas of Sergiev Posad, matryoshka making centres started to spring up in Russia.

T. Zelova
12-piece matryoshka
'Palekh Motifs'
Khotkovo. 1996

A. Melnikovich, O. Bolhova
10-piece matryoshka **'Lace'**
Khotkovo. 1996

Usually, these were old Russian centres of folk arts and crafts and mainly turning skills. Possibly, the craftsmen could see a new doll, matryoshka, at fairs. The biggest fair was held at Nizhny Novgorod. Matryoshka making centres appeared in the area of Nizhny Novgorod.

Semionov town became quite a big matryoshka making centre. This type of matryoshka is called Semionovskaya.

Among contributors to the matryoshkas of Semionov are the Mayorovs. They were a toy making family from the village of Merinovo, located near Semionov. The masters of Merinovo were always famous for their turning wares. They made wooden utensils, rattles, balls and apples. In 1922 Arsenty Fedorovich Mayorov brought an unpainted matryoshka from the fair

N. Antonova
Sugar Bowl **'The Owner'**
Sergiev Posad. 1996
Private collection

N. Antonova
5-piece matryoshka **'The family'**
5-piece matryoshka **'The Owner'**
5-piece matryoshka **'The Owner'**
Sergiev Posad. 1993-1994
Private collection

in Nizhny Novgorod. His elder daughter Luba used a quill to make an outline and coloured it with red dye. She placed a bright red flower resembling an ox-eye daisy in the centre. She painted a kokoshnik on the matryoshka's head. Almost twenty years the matryoshka makers of Merinovo were the best in the area of Nizhny Novgorod.

In 1931 an artel which made souvenirs including matryoshkas was established in Semionov.

Gradually a distinct matryoshka type of Semionov was developed. It was more decorative and symbolic than the matryoshkas of Sergiev Posad. Semionov's traditions go back to the floral ornament of ancient Russia. The painters of Semionov used aniline dyes. They left quite a lot of unpainted space and varnished matryoshkas. First of all, light touches of the brush mark the outlines of the face, eyes, the lines of the lips and apply colour to the cheeks. Then a skirt, an apron, a scarf on the matryoshka's head and hands are drawn.

An apron is considered to be the main thing in painting of Semionov. A bright bouquet of flowers is painted on it. It is possible to recognise the technique of old Russian masters. The early matryoshkas of Semionov were more in the spirit of old Russian painting traditions, the lines were more graphic and lighter. Later the bouquet was suffused with the sap of the grass, and became more dense, colourful and graphic. At present, three colours predominate in the deco-

M. Yakimova
Sugar Bowl **'Hunting'**
Pushkino. 1996

A. *Kartashov*
10-piece matryoshka **'Yaroslavna'**
(with a fragment)
Sergiev Posad. 1993
Private collection

ON PAGE 50:
M. Masaltseva
5-piece matryoshka
'Saint Tsar's Family'
Moscow. 1991
Private collection

rations — red, blue and yellow which appear in various combinations in the scarf, sarafan and apron. The colour solution of the bouquet is the main feature in the matryoshkas of Semionov. It sets the tone for the whole colour scheme. Traditionally, the bouquet is painted on the apron

A. Beketov
10-piece matryoshka **'Biblical'**
(with fragments)
Sochi. 1995
Private collection

asymmetrically, bit to the right of the centre. The decoration of the matryoshkas of Semionov is original and unique. A painter brings something new to each matryoshka style. The matryoshkas of the Volga area bear an imprint of ancient, folk culture which is developed by modern craftsmen. The turners of Semionov invented their own shape of matryoshka which differs from the matryoshkas of Sergiev Posad. It is more slender, it has a relatively thin top which widens sharply into a thick bottom.

The matryoshkas of Semionov are famous for containing many pieces (15-18 varicoloured dolls). The biggest matryoshka which contains 72 pieces—0.5 m (1.5 feet) in diameter and 1 m (3 feet) high—was turned in Semionov.

'Russian Lad' and 'Russian Lass' twin matryoshkas are very original. They are more slen-

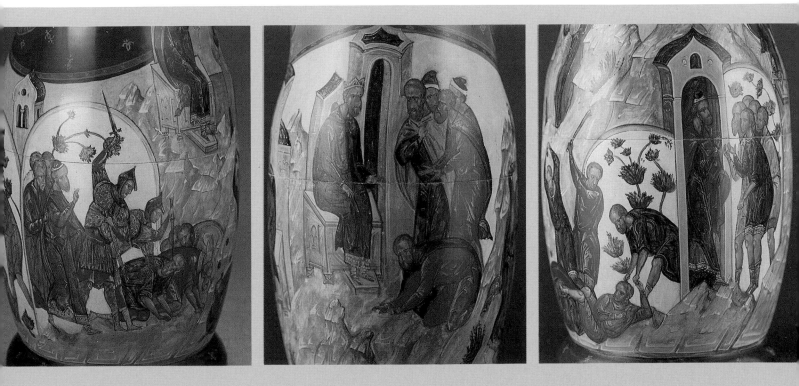

N. Antonova
4-piece matryoshka
'A Tiny Berry'
Sergiev Posad. 1993

M. Nadezhdina
Egg-shaped matryoshka
'In the Boat'
Khotkovo. 1993

M. Yakimova
6-piece matryoshka **'Granny'**
Pushkino. 1992

der than usual matryoshkas of Semionov, dressed in traditional Russian costumes: the lass wears a scarf instead of kokoshnik and the lad wears a peaked cap.

'The Russian woman', 'The Good Family Man', 'The Russian Lad' and others are famous matryoshkas of Semionov. The craftsmen turned and painted matryoshkas at home till 1929. Then the craftsmen of Semionov and nearby villages formed a toy-making artel. Initially it included not more than 20 people. Now souvenir workshops of Semionov are the biggest centre in Russia where matryoshkas are made.

Polkhovsky Maidan, located to the southwest of Nizhny Novgorod, is another matryoshka making centre.

Wooden workmanship was an old tradition there. Many toys were made on a turning lathe: samovars, birds, money-box, salt-cellars and ap-

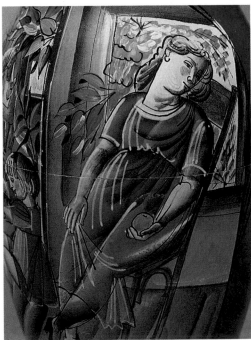

V. Bulygina
12-piece matryoshka
'Khotkovo'
(with fragments)
Khotkovo. 1983

N. Suslova
10-piece matryoshka **'My Wedding'**
(with fragments)
Khotkovo. 1990

ples. The first matriohskas of Polkhovsky Maidan like the matryoshkas of Sergiev Posad were made by poker-work, then local craftsmen started to paint wooden dolls with floral ornaments. The craftsmen of Polkhovsky Maidan like the craftsmen of Semionov use aniline dyes. The matryoshkas were pasted over, brightly painted before being coated with varnish. The colours of the matryoshkas of Polkhovsky Maidan are brighter and more expressive than the colours of the matryoshkas of Semionov, their ornaments are bigger as well. Green, blue, yellow, violet and crimson colours are used to contrast each other, to make an expressive and bright ornament. Richness of colour is achieved by superimposing one layer of dye on another.

The matryoshkas of Polkhovsky. Maidan are manufactured in the peasant primitive style which resembles children's drawings. It is a typical village beauty with knitted brows and a face framed in black locks. The ringlets of hair are a genuine element of local women's head-dress.

Older women covered their hair with ko-koshniks, young girls used ribbons. Black drake's feathers were stuck in their head- dress-es. The painters of Polkhovsky Maidan as the painters of Semionov paid their special attention to floral ornament of matryoshkas' aprons. They ignored other details of a matryoshka's cos-tume. Dog-rose with many petals is the main ele-ment of apron painting. This flower is always con-sidered to be the symbol of femininity, love and motherhood.

This flower is a part of each composition of the craftsmen of Polkhovsky Maidan. Some-times this theme is developed and a painter adds to the main rose its buds on the branches.

Craftsmen of the village of Krutets, located in the same area, started to paint wooden turned

M. Masaltseva
5-piece matryoshka
'Children's Dreams'
Moscow. 1992

N. Suslova
5-piece matryoshka
**'Easter and How We Were
Looking Forward to It'**
Khotkovo. 1989

M. Masaltseva
3-piece matryoshka
**'Once Upon a Time,
There Was a Girl'.** 1989
3-piece matryoshka **'Dacha'.** 1993
Moscow, private collection

ON PAGE 60:
Craftsman Leonova
Matryoshka-little family (7-pieces)
'Behind the Outskirts'
Sergiev Posad. Early 1990s

L. Lebedeva
7-piece matryoshka
**'A Nothern Wedding
Costume'**
Moscow. 1996

toys including matryoshkas as well. The matryoshkas made in Krutets differ by greater varity of themes and ornaments. They are quite experimental. This applies not only to decoration but also to the shape.

Matryoshka of Vyatka is the most northern Russian matryoshka. It portrays blue eyed girl from the North with a gentle bashful smile. The girl's face is so charming that it attracts everyone. The painted dolls of Vyatka became especially original in the 1960s, when the matryoshkas were painted not only by aniline dyes but inlaid with straw. Then the straw is covered by oil lacquer.

On PAGE *62, 63:*
M. Petrova
10-piece matryoshka **'Winter'**
(with fragments)
Sergiev Posad. 1994
Private collection

S. Gorbacheva
5-piece matryoshka **'Christmas'**
Sergiev Posad. 1995
Private collection

Nolinskaya souvenir factory and Kirovskaya souvenir factory are the parts of Vyatka amalgamation. Matryoshka 'Sudarushka' produced by Nolinskaya factory is very popular.

Possibly, a painted matryoshka will remain one of the most vivid relics of the late 1980s and early 1990s in Russia. The third period of matryoshka art development starts from this time. This period is called a period of author's mat-

ryoshkas. This was revolutionary time fraught with serious changes

The economic, social and cultural changes that began in Russia, the famous Gorbachev perestroika caused the great interest in Russian culture all over the world. Russian matryoshka had a Renaissance as well. Like 100 years ago independent workshops and co-operatives where matryoshkas were made were opened.

Craftsmen got the opportunity to sell their matryoshkas. Russian art market experienced unbelievable upsurge. Matryoshkas prevailed among the pieces of art on the market. Professional artists were among those who started painting matryoshkas: painters, pencil artists, masters of folk art handicrafts.

The most popular matryoshka was author's matryoshka which was different from traditional

I. Rebrov
9-piece matryoshka
'Abstract'
Moscow. 1989

I. Rebrov
9-piece matryoshka
'Blue Morning'
7-piece matryoshka
'Summer'
Moscow. 1989

L. Merkulova
12-piece matryoshka **'Hunting'**
(with fragments)
Moscow. 1994
Private collection

styles. It was made by an individual artist, whether professional or amateur one. The typical matryoshka which had been worked out during the Soviet time was replaced by matryoshkas whose decoration could be described as 'individual anarchy'.

The matryoshka makers brought back the variety of themes in matryoshka painting which existed in Sergiev Posad period.

Different matryoshkas portrayed again Russian peasant girls which resembled the first Russian matryoshka made by Maliutin. The traditional type of the matryoshkas of Sergiev Posad which usually hold something in their hands was complemented by a variety of women, young girls, old women with baskets full of fruits, samovars, bast-baskets, all sorts of dippers and pitchers.

Artistic method of contemporary matryoshka makers was more decorative in comparison with the early samples of the matryoshkas of Sergiev Posad. The objects held by matryoshkas turned into special still-lives. The image of the matryoshka with a big family came back as well.

Matryoshka owner which holds some kind of fowl, for example, a goose or a piglet, belonged to this type as well.

The family theme is linked with motherhood theme. The first craftsmen who painted matryoshkas as mothers holding their babies were the craftsmen of Krutets. The craftsmen of Sergiev Posad of the early period didn't

O. Simukhina (*painting*)
S. Simukhin (*fashioning*)
10-piece matryoshka
'Hunting'
Sergiev Posad. 1993
Private collection

I. Andrianov
10-piece matryoshka
'The Lay of Igor's Host'
Sergiev Posad. 1993
Private collection

I. Gvozdevskaya, I. Vatrushkina
7-piece matryoshka
'A Village Family'
5-piece matryoshka
'Russian Restaurant'
(with fragments)
Gzhel. 1996

have this painting tradition but during the period of author's matryoshka this tradition was developed a lot. Very interesting samples appeared in Moscow, Sergiev Posad and Khotkovo. Motherhood theme is linked with the idea of peace, comfort and protection; lullaby sung before sleep, wonderful fairy tales. Mary the Virgin who was always greatly venerated in Russian is an ideal for each mother image. Gradually,

L. Tretiakova
15-piece matryoshka
'Mishka's Name Day'
Sergiev Posad. 1996

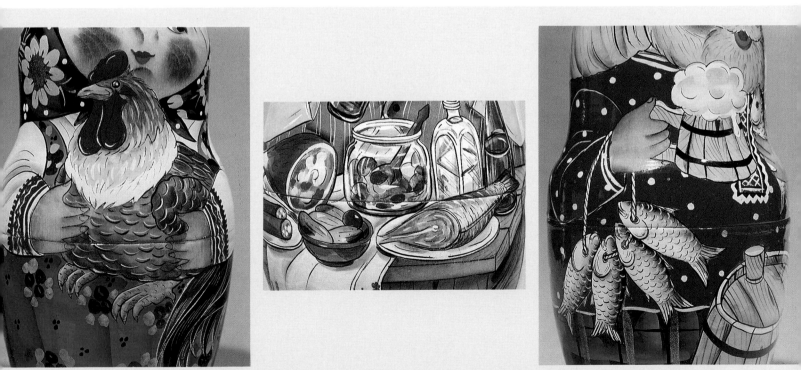

ON PAGE 74, 75:
E. Gorbachev, S. Gorbacheva
15-piece matryoshka
'Zhostovo Tray'
(with fragments)
Sergiev Posad. 1994
Private collection

some artists portrayed Mary the Virgin with infant Jesus instead of some concrete image of mother. It is connected with the revival of the religious feeling and Orthodoxy. At the beginning of the 20th century many icon painters of Sergiev Posad started to decorate matryoshkas.

They could not break certain icon painting canons. That's why the first matryoshka painters who had icon painting experience were happy to

portray their contemporaries. The artists could observe them everyday on the busy streets of Sergiev Posad. The methods and themes of secular painting could not be used in icons, so they develop their creative potential in decoration of wooden dolls.

The matryoshkas of the early period portray different inhabitants of pre-Revolutionary Russia.

L. Pertseva
5-piece matryoshka
'Dearie'
Moscow. 1996

If at the beginning of the 20th century there was a trend away from icon painting traditions towards realistic portrayal, then in 1990s matryoshka craftsmen came closer to icon style again. Gradually, some of them started to decorate Easter eggs and then to paint icons.

The former icon painters' descendants are getting back to the traditional activity of their ancestors. For examples 'Yaroslavna' of

A. Kartashov: Yaroslavna, the wife of the legendary Russian prince Igor Sviatoslavovich is portrayed holding the icon of Mary the Virgin of Vladimir in her hands. This matryoshka is painted in a very noble way. As a rule in order to portray Mary the Virgin, Jesus Christ, apostles and saints, artists used icon painting techniques. They consider matryoshka as some kind of a surface on which they draw an icon, not as a doll to be dressed in clothes of a saint.

J. Gavrilenko, A. Gavrilenko
11-piece matryoshka
'A Party' (with fragments)
Sergiev Posad. 1993
Private collection

The characteristic feature of the contemporary author's matryoshka is its picturesqueness.

Often the constructive principle of matryoshka doll is sacrificed for the general decorative pattern. The whole painting resembles a variegated fabric and looks very festive. The world around us seen nostalgically by the painter becomes a major theme. To many people living in Russia their country turned to be something new, unusual and at some point mysterious. Icon paintings and Christmas holidays — Easter and Christmas, rituals of christening and church wedding became popular and legitimate again.

In the true folk environment all customs and holidays have never been excluded from the spiritual and cultural traditions which were preserved from generation to generation. At the beginning of 1990s this part of life became public. Some painters tried to reflect these trends in their decorated matryoshkas. In the portrayal of their birthplace they appreciate the new value of it in the historic context. For example, 'Khotkovo'

81

T. Volkova
5-piece matryoshka **'The Garden of Eden'**
(with a fragment)
Sergiev Posad. 1995

by V. Bulygina and 'Abramtsevo Nights' by O. Kiseliova belong to this type. It is important to note that not only the views of their native villages reflect their view of the whole world but they see themselves as part of this world. For example, matryoshka 'My wedding' by V. Bulygina, portraying the beautiful ritual of church wedding, reflects some features of the author as well.

The inquisitive eye of the painter strives to penetrate in the past, the present and the future. Due to the rising national identity, a modern painter tries to understand customs and traditions of ancestors. If the masters of the early period found some themes for the decoration of their matryoshkas in the surrounded world, the author's matryoshka is distinguished by a certain 'documentary' aspect, supported by old photographs and documents.

The artist is looking attentively at the meaningful faces and poses of his ancestors and tries to understand their style of life. For example, the artists M. Masaltseva and N. Suslova work in

T. Volkova
5-piece matryoshka
'English Fairy Tale'
(with a fragment).
Sergiev Posad. 1995

this way. The theme of Easter, one of the most revered by Russians Orthodox holidays is conveyed with love and affection by N. Suslova in her matryoshka 'Easter and How We Were Looking Forward to It'. We see how the artist passionately conveys through the matryoshka decoration the emotional evaluation of the events.

The history of this country from Prince Igor's campaign to the contemporary political struggle is

On PAGE 84:
E. Zhilkina
8-piece matryoshka
'Moon Fairy Tale'
Moscow. 1993

On PAGE 85:
O. Simukhina (painting)
S. Simukhin (fashioning)
6-piece matryoshka
'The Nutcracker'
Sergiev Posad. 1993
Private collection

M. Yakimova
4-piece matryoshka
'Apostles'
Pushkino. 1990
Private collection

represented by matryoshkas. One of the most popular themes at that time was the tragedy of the Tsar's family. The historical evidence and historians' publications shocked the society by cynicism and cruelty of what had been committed. The last

N. Chupina
10-piece matryoshka
'Characters of Russian Folklore'
Moscow. 1996

days of Nicholas II and his family were featured in films, books, and plays. The matryoshkas portrayed the members of the family as well.

We experience very difficult time: we used to live in the country of certain economic structure and quite imperceptibly we are living in the state professing completely different economic principles. It is quite natural that all these radical changes are accompanied with the breaking of the ideals, life's cataclysms breaking in people's consciousness. At the same time, a lot of things in our life resemble an old classic vaudeville

which is a bit absurd. Sometimes our life resembles a noisy motley carnival in Venice where the seriousness and fun, tragedy and comedy, banality and mystery are mixed.

Matryoshka, a doll which looks quite simple but full of unexpected sense turned out to be the best embodiment of the present time spirit. Matryoshka as a form of folk art possesses tremendous potential to convey the deepest sense of the events developed in space and time. The carnival folk element which is seen in the matryoshka decoration allows not only to rise life's eternal issues, but to realise contemporary life in its every day and busy form.

For example, these is the whole range of Russian tsars, Russian and foreign state and public officials. The matryoshkas portraying modern politicians have a grotesque style—old tradition

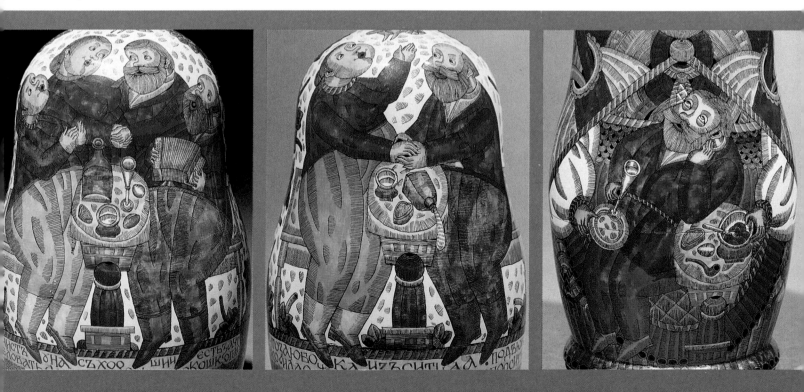

appeared long time ago. For example, a very well known matryoshka- caricature was painted by V. A. Serov. S. I. Mamontov, V. A. Serov himself, musicians P. A. Spiro, N. A. Rimsky-Korsakov and other participants of the Mamontovs theatrical performances were represented in Turkish costumes.

Almost all political upheavals of the late 1980s and the early 1990s are represented in

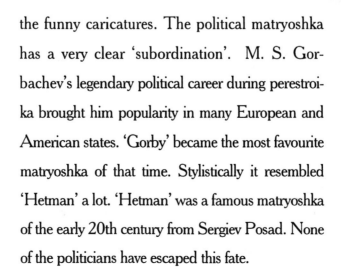

the funny caricatures. The political matryoshka has a very clear 'subordination'. M. S. Gorbachev's legendary political career during perestroika brought him popularity in many European and American states. 'Gorby' became the most favourite matryoshka of that time. Stylistically it resembled 'Hetman' a lot. 'Hetman' was a famous matryoshka of the early 20th century from Sergiev Posad. None of the politicians have escaped this fate.

A. Zusina
9-piece matryoshka with kids
9-piece matryoshka with kids
5-piece matryoshka with a cat
5-piece matryoshka with kids
Moscow. 1995

A special order was made in Russia to portray the future US president and his closest aids in the framework of Bill Clinton's inauguration.

Long time ago at the beginning of the 20th century some painters tried to use matryoshka as a surface to paint some pictures on it. It could be either fairy tale theme or a landscape. These attempts made in the past helped to develop a new matryoshka type.

Its wooden form is used to reproduce this or that theme. Two traditions in matryoshka painting are linked with each other: the topicality of Sergiev Posad painting joins the decorative manner of Nizhny Novgorod. Matryoshka's apron is a traditional place to feature the major element in the matryoshkas of Nizhny Novgorod. This particular detail is borrowed by modern toy makers.

Various types of matryoshkas are distinguished by the way their aprons are painted. For example, some matryoshkas have architectural monuments on their aprons. Such matryoshka is a wonderful souvenir which reminds this or that historical place.

Matryoshkas representing Trinity - St. Sergius Monastery, architectural monuments of the

M. Nadezhdina
10-piece matryoshka
'The Village Summer'
(with fragments)
Khotkovo. 1993
Private collection

old Russian towns of Vladimir, Suzdal, Novgorod and other are very popular.

The trend of using decorative elements which are typical for Russian folk culture traditional centres becomes more and more popular in the decoration of modern matryoshka. Very often one can see a matryoshka painted a la gzel, zhostovo, khokhloma, palekh.

Modern matryoshka absorbs in a certain ways the treasures of folk Russian art traditions. Author's matryoshkas are very expressive and energetic.

It is quite natural in the late 1980s and early 1990s that many Russian professional artists and craftsman earlier deprived by certain barriers started to paint matryoshkas. This type of art revealed their energy which had been preserved for along time. The matryoshkas painting imbibes all bright, fresh elements connected with the renewal and the renaissance of Russian society of the 20th century.

It is possible to say that this time has given the world the new art—Russian author's painted matryoshka

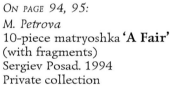

On page 94, 95:
M. Petrova
10-piece matryoshka **'A Fair'**
(with fragments)
Sergiev Posad. 1994
Private collection

which is a part of many Russian and Western art collections.

We can see dignity and humility, power and hope for the future, deep sorrow and boundless hilarity in the Russian painted matryoshka... Time goes on and the new generations are impressed by the talent and imagination of the creators of folk and author's matryoshkas, they derive vital force for the quest and achievments from this source.

Matryoshka is a huge artistic event which requires comprehension. It is both sculpture and painting, image and soul of Russia.

Russian Souvenir

Larisa Soloviova

Russian matryoshka

Album

Director: *Gennady Popov*
Redactor: *Nadezhda Fedorova*
Computer operator: *Tatiana Anosova*
Computer lay-out: *Vladimir Bortnikov*

The book has been prepared for publication by
Interbook Business Publishers
Publishing license LR N 071222 05.10.1995

To establish co-operation and to purchase books, please,
contact:
Office 11, 12/9 Spiridonievsky Pereulok
Moscow, 103104, Russia
Phone: (095) 200-64-62
Fax: (095) 956-37-52